D0605178

First Ladies

Abigail Adams

Launch!
An Imprint of Abdo Zoom
abdopublishing.com

Jennifer Strand

abdopublishing.com

Published by Abdo Zoom, a division of ABDO, PO Box 398166, Minneapolis, Minnesota 55439.
Copyright © 2019 by Abdo Consulting Group, Inc. International copyrights reserved in all countries.
No part of this book may be reproduced in any form without written permission from the publisher.
Launch!™ is a trademark and logo of Abdo Zoom.

Printed in the United States of America, North Mankato, Minnesota.

052018
092018

**THIS BOOK CONTAINS
RECYCLED MATERIALS**

Photo Credits: Alamy, Granger, Shutterstock

Production Contributors: Kenny Abdo, Jennie Forsberg, Grace Hansen, John Hansen

Design Contributors: Dorothy Toth, Neil Klinepier

Library of Congress Control Number: 2017960494

Publisher's Cataloging-in-Publication Data

Names: Strand, Jennifer, author.

Title: Abigail Adams / by Jennifer Strand.

Description: Minneapolis, Minnesota : Abdo Zoom, 2019. | Series: First ladies |
    Includes online resources and index.

Identifiers: ISBN 9781532122811 (lib.bdg.) | ISBN 9781532123795 (ebook) |
    ISBN 9781532124280 (Read-to-me ebook)

Subjects: LCSH: Adams, Abigail 1744-1818--Biography--Juvenile literature. | Presidents' spouses--United
    States--Biography--Juvenile literature. | First ladies (United States)--Biography--Juvenile literature.

Classification: DDC 973.44092 [B]--dc23

Table of Contents

Introduction

Abigail Adams was a First Lady of the United States. Her husband John Adams was the second president of the United States.

She was the first woman to live in the White House.

Early Life

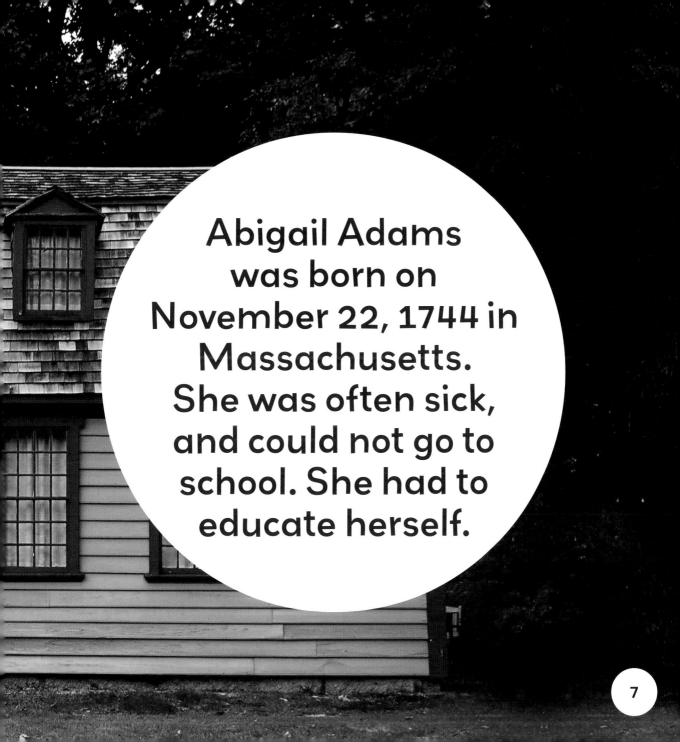

Abigail Adams was born on November 22, 1744 in Massachusetts. She was often sick, and could not go to school. She had to educate herself.

In 1764 she married John Adams. He was a lawmaker in the **Revolutionary War.**

They had 6 children, including future president John Quincy Adams.

Leader

Adams ran the household and family farm while John was away on work.

She would write him regularly. The letters were about political issues of the day.

Adams also ran businesses. She bought land and dealt with **tenants**.

First Lady

Adams was First Lady from 1797 to 1801. She was a strong supporter of women's **rights**.

15

Adams knew about key issues. Her husband came to her for advice. She was so active, her opponents called her "Mrs. President."

Legacy

Abigail Adams is remembered for her support of women's **rights**, religious freedom, and the end to **slavery**.

19

Abigail Adams

Born: November 22, 1744

Birthplace: Weymouth, Massachusetts

Husband: John Adams

Years Served: 1797-1801

Political Party: Federalist

Known For: Adams was the second US First Lady. She wrote many letters that revealed her strong political and social opinions.

Key Dates

1744: Abigail Smith is born on November 22.

1764: Abigail marries John Adams.

1784–1788: Abigail lives in Europe while her husband is a **diplomat**.

1789–1797: Abigail Adams is Second Lady. John Adams is the first vice president.

1797–1801: Abigail Adams is First Lady. John Adams is the second US president.

1818: Abigail dies on October 28.

Glossary

diplomat – a person who officially represents a country's interests abroad.

Revolutionary War – a war fought between England and the North American colonies from 1775 to 1783.

rights – things people can have or do according to the law.

slavery – the practice of owning people. A slave is a person who is bought and sold as property.

tenant – a person who stays on land or property rented from a landlord.

Online Resources

For more information on
Abigail Adams, please visit
abdobooklinks.com

Learn even more with the
Abdo Zoom Biographies database.
Visit **abdozoom.com** today!

Index